EASY PIANO

SMASH POP HITS 2001

ARRANGED BY DAN COATES & RICHARD BRADLEY

W9-AUF-644

Project Manager: CAROL CUELLAR
Art Design: KEN REHM

CONTENTS

BABYLON

Words and Music by
DAVID GRAY
Arranged by RICHARD BRADLEY

Moderately bright ($\downarrow$ = 112)

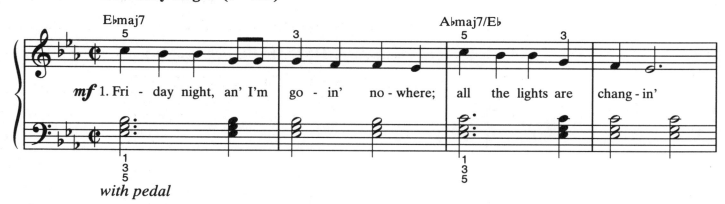

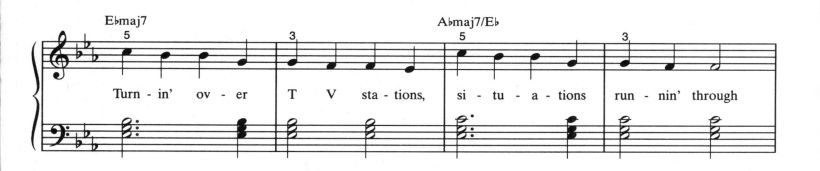

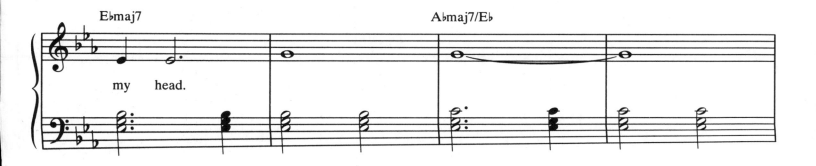

4

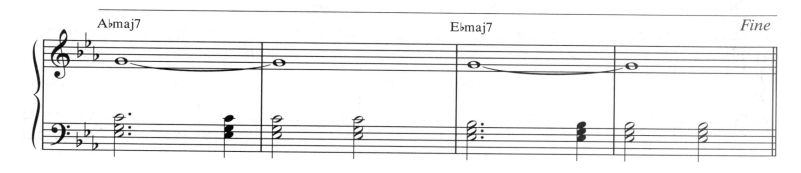

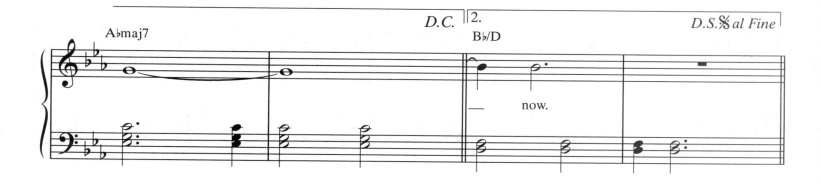

Verse 2:
Saturday, I'm runnin' wild,
An' all the lights are changin' red to green.
Movin' through the crowds, I'm pushin';
Chemicals are rushin' in my bloodstream.
Only wish that you were here,
You know I'm seein' it so clear;
I've been afraid to show you how I really feel,
Admit to some of those bad mistakes I've made.

Verse 3:
Sunday, all the lights in London shining,
Sky is fading red to blue.
Kickin' through the autumn leaves
An' wonderin' where it is you might be goin' to.
Turnin' back for home,
You know I'm feelin' so alone I can't believe.
Climbin' on the stair, I turn around
To see you smilin' there in front of me.

AMERICAN PIE

Words and Music by
DON McLEAN
Arranged by DAN COATES

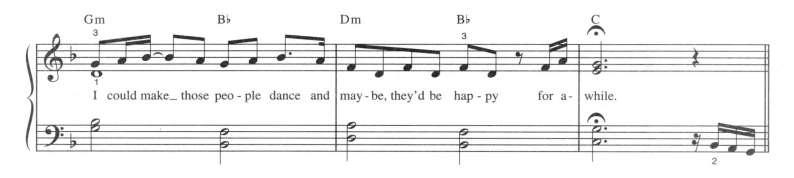

Bright, steady beat
Verse:

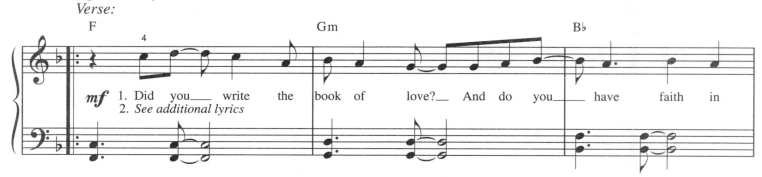

American Pie - 4 - 1

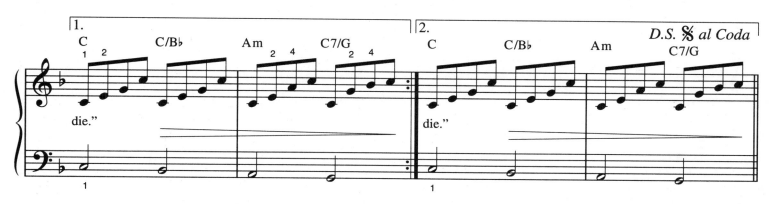

Verse 2:
I met a girl who sang the blues
And I asked her for some happy news,
But she just smiled and turned away.
I went down to the sacred store,
Where I heard the music years before,
But the man there said the music wouldn't play.
And in the streets, the children screamed,
The lovers cried and the poets dreamed.
But not a word was spoken;
The church bells were all broken.
And the three men I admire most,
The Father, Son, and Holy Ghost,
They caught the last train for the coast
The day the music died.
And they were singin':
(To Chorus:)

CAN'T FIGHT THE MOONLIGHT
(Theme from Coyote Ugly)

Words and Music by
DIANE WARREN
Arranged by DAN COATES

Moderate, steady beat (♩ = 98)

Verse:

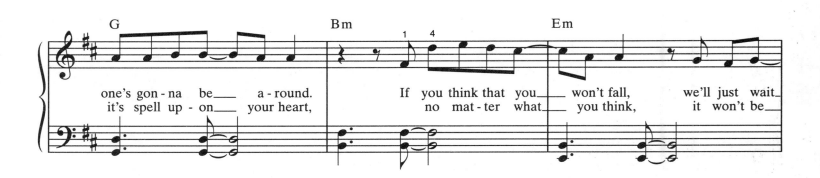

one's gon-na be___ a-round.
it's spell up-on___ your heart,

If you think that you___ won't fall,
no mat-ter what___ you think,

we'll just wait,
it won't be

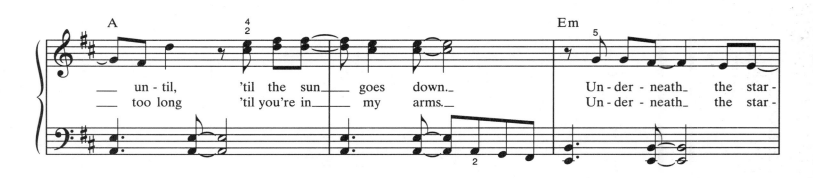

___ un-til, 'til the sun___ goes down.
___ too long 'til you're in___ my arms.

Un-der-neath___ the star-
Un-der-neath___ the star-

light, star-light,___ there's a mag-i-cal feel-ing so___ right.
light, star-light,___ we'll be lost___ in a rhy-thm so___ right.

Bridge:

Chorus:

to re - sist,___ try to hide___ from my kiss,___ but you know,___ but you know___ that you

can't fight the moon - light. Deep___ in the dark,___ you'll sur - ren - der your heart.__ Don't you know,___

___ don't you know___ that you   can't fight the moon - light,   no,   you can't fight___

___ it.   You can try___ ___ it.   It's gon-na get to your   heart.___

COME ON OVER
(ALL I WANT IS YOU)

Words and Music by
PAUL REIN and JOHAN ABERG
Arranged by DAN COATES

Come on Over - 4 - 1

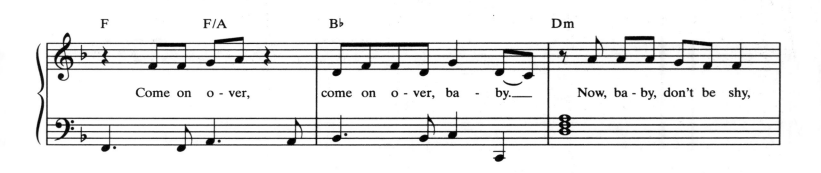

Chorus:

All I want is you.

All I want is you. Now, ba - by, don't be shy, you bet - ter cross the line.

I'm gon - na love you right 'cause all I, all I want is | all I want is you.

Verse 2:
I want you to know,
You could be the one for me, yes, you could.
You've got all I'm looking for,
You've got personality.
I know, you know, I'm gonna give you more.
The things you do,
I've never felt this way before.
So, boy, won't you come,
Won't you come and open my door?
Listen to me.
(To Chorus:)

BREATHLESS

Words and Music by
JAMES CORR, SHARON CORR,
CAROLINE CORR, ANDREA CORR and R.J. LANGE
Arranged by RICHARD BRADLEY

Moderate rock (♩ = 96)

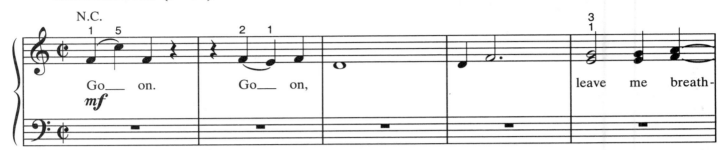

Go___ on. Go___ on, leave me breath-

less.___

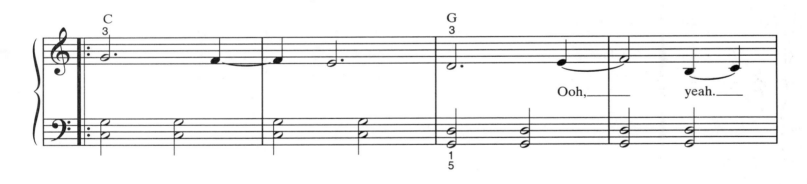

Ooh,___ yeah.___

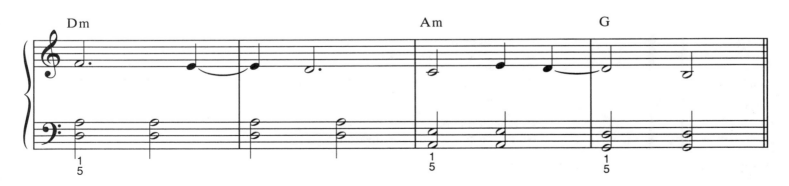

Breathless - 5 - 1

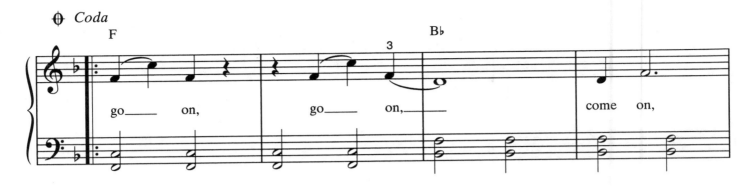

go___ on, go___ on,___ come on,

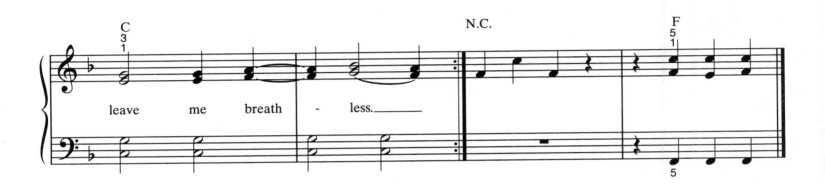

leave me breath - less.___

Verse 2:
And if there's no tomorrow,
And all we have is here and now,
I'm happy just to have you.
You're all the love I need somehow.
It's like a dream, although I'm not asleep.
I never want to wake up.
Don't lose it. Don't leave it.

Verse 3:
And I cannot lie, from you I cannot hide.
And I've lost my will to try.
Can't hide it. Can't fight it.

DARE TO DREAM

Words and Music by
PAUL BEGAUD, VANESSA CORISH
and WAYNE TESTER
Arranged by DAN COATES

Moderately slow (♩ = 72)

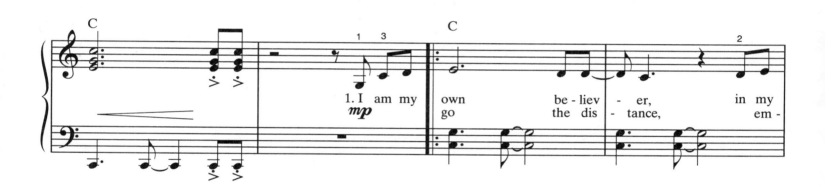

Dare to Dream - 5 - 1

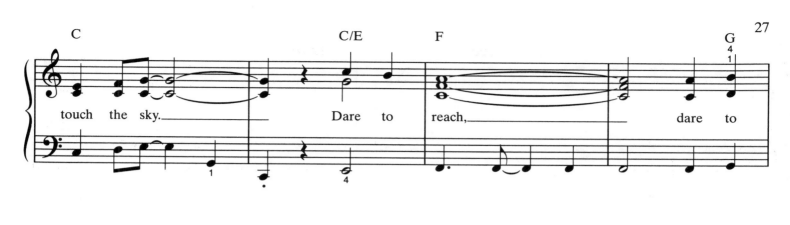

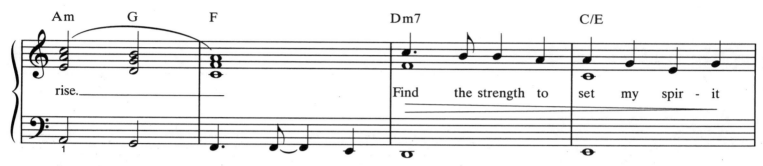

Dare to Dream - 5 - 3

FOR MY WEDDING

Words and Music by
LARRY JOHN McNALLY
Arranged by DAN COATES

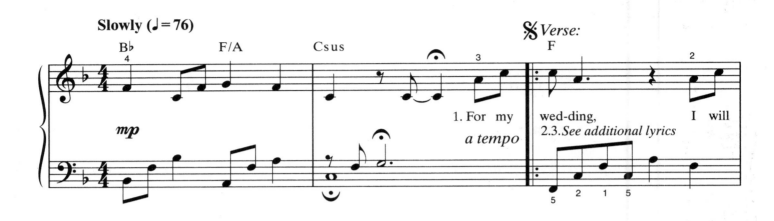

For My Wedding - 3 - 1

been that way,___ well, I can dream___ and I can pray___

D.S. % al Coda

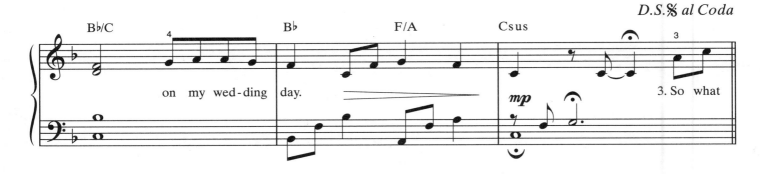

on my wed-ding day. *mp* 3. So what

Coda

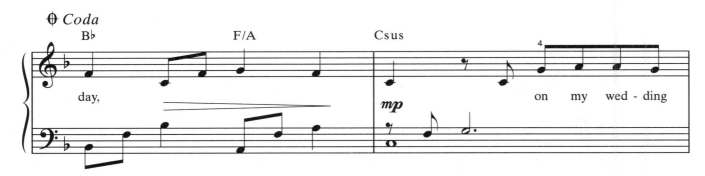

day, *mp* on my wed-ding

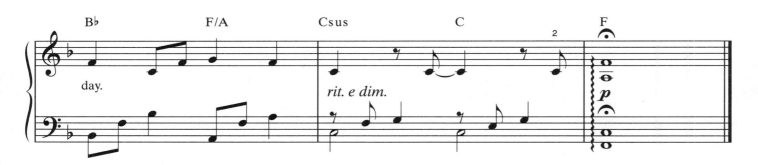

day. *rit. e dim.*

Verse 2:
For my wedding, I don't want violins
Or sentimental songs about thick and thin.
I want a moment of silence and a moment of prayer
For the love we'll need to make it in the world out there.
(To Chorus:)

Verse 3:
So what makes us any different from all the others
Who have tried and failed before us?
Maybe nothing, maybe nothing at all.
But I pray we're the lucky ones; I pray we'll never fall.
(To Chorus:)

GIVE ME JUST ONE NIGHT
(UNA NOCHE)

Words and Music by
CLAUDIA OGALDE, ANDERS BAGGE
and ARNTHOR BIRGISSON
Arranged by DAN COATES

Moderately fast (♩ = 124)

Verse 1:

1. Your lips keep tell-ing me you want me,_____ and hold me close all through the night. And I know____ that deep in-side you need me._____

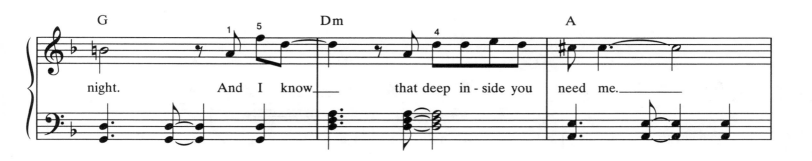

Verses 2 & 3:

No one else can make it right.
2. Don't you try to hide your
3. Your eyes with pas-sion make me

Give Me Just One Night - 3 - 1

I'll give you the time of your life.

To Coda

Give me just one

D.S. al Coda

Coda

HERE WITH ME
(Theme From Roswell)

Words and Music by
PAUL STATHAM, PASCAL GABRIEL
and DIDO ARMSTRONG

Moderately slow (♩ = 88)

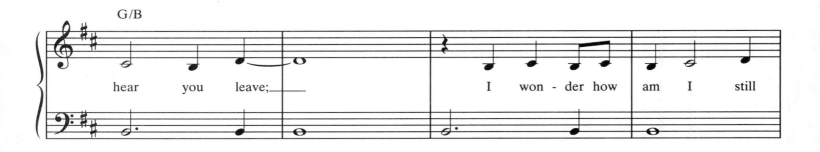

Here With Me - 5 - 1

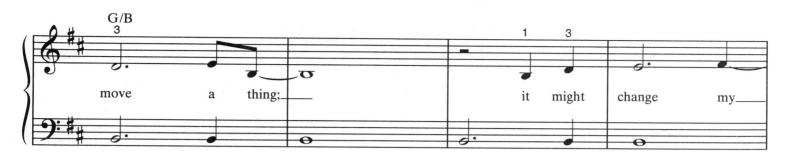

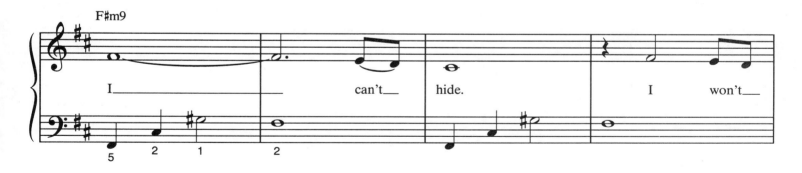

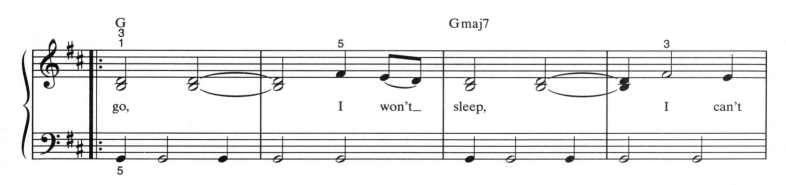

Here With Me - 5 - 2

38

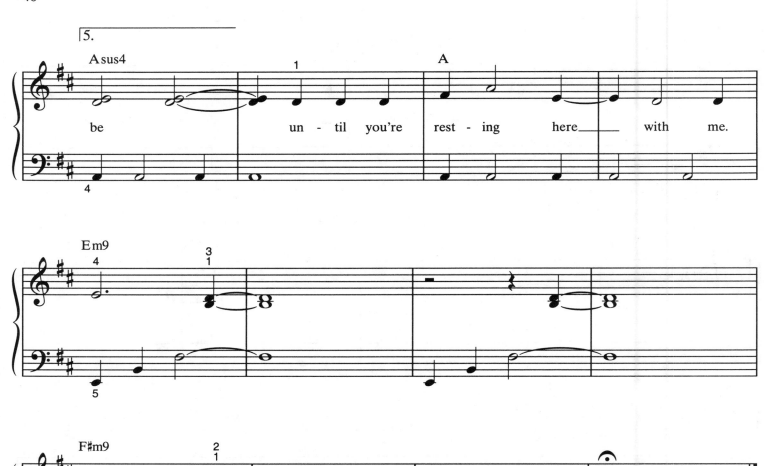

Verse 2:
I don't want to call my friends;
They might wake me from this dream.
I can't leave this bed,
Risk of frogetting all that's been.

I BELIEVE

Words and Music by
ERIC LEVI
Arranged by DAN COATES

Slowly, with expression

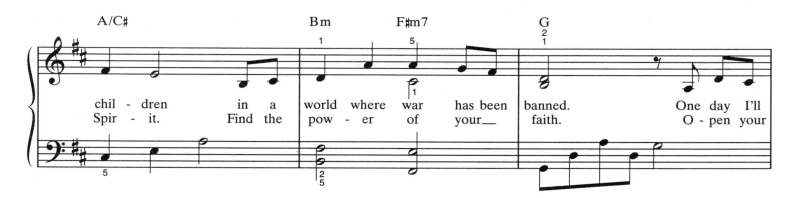

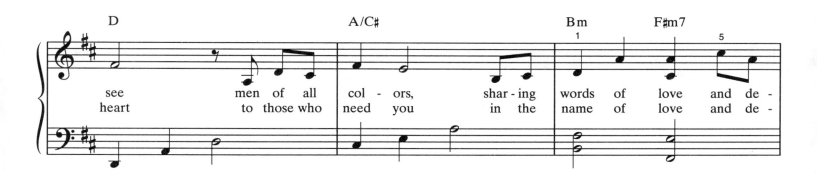

I Believe - 5 - 1

2.

Yes, I be - lieve. I be-lieve in the

Chorus:

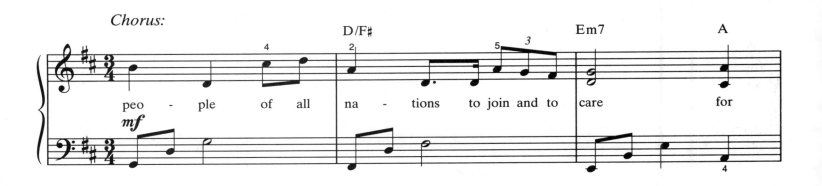

peo - ple of all na - tions to join and to care for

love. I be-lieve in a world where light will guide us. And giv - ing our

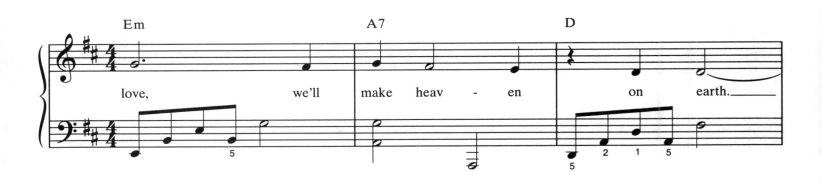

love, we'll make heav - en on earth.

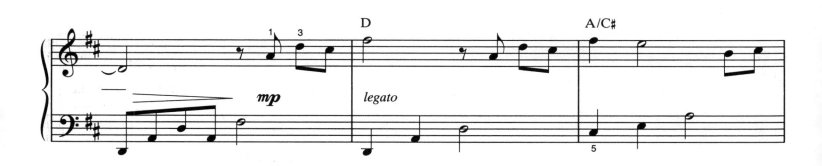

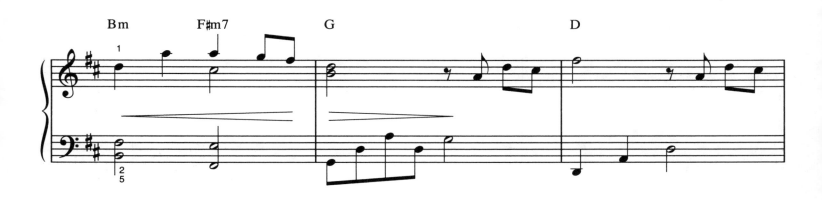

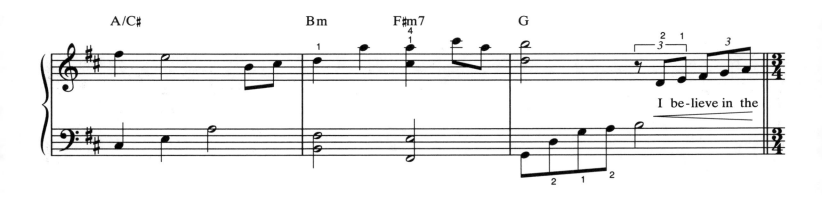

I be-lieve in the

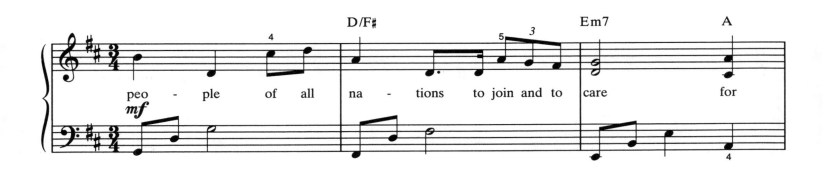

peo - ple of all na - tions to join and to care for

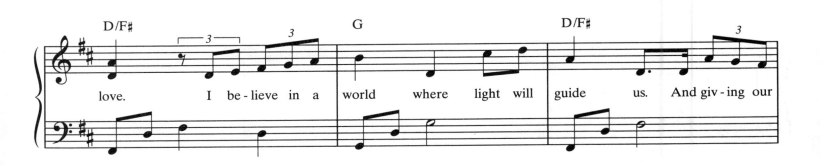

love. I be-lieve in a world where light will guide us. And giv-ing our

love, we'll make___ heav - en on earth.

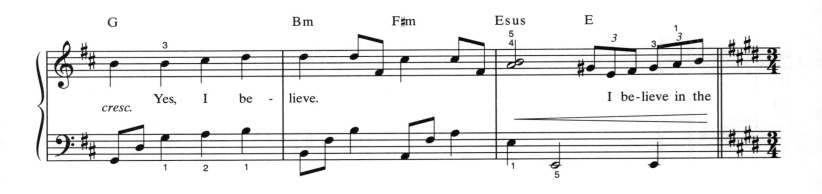

cresc. Yes, I be - lieve. I be-lieve in the

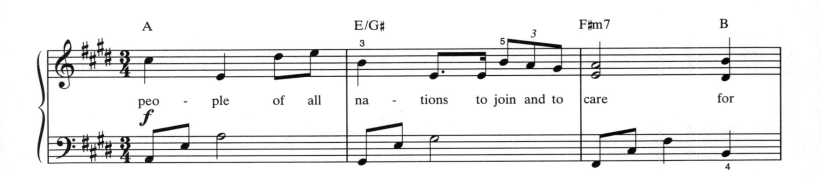

peo - ple of all na - tions to join and to care for

45

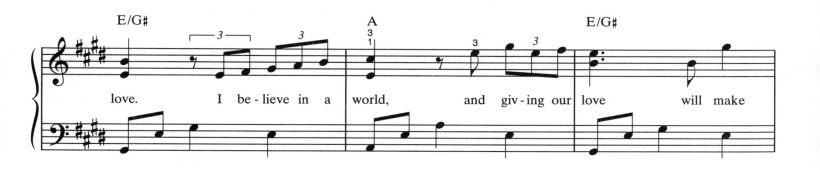

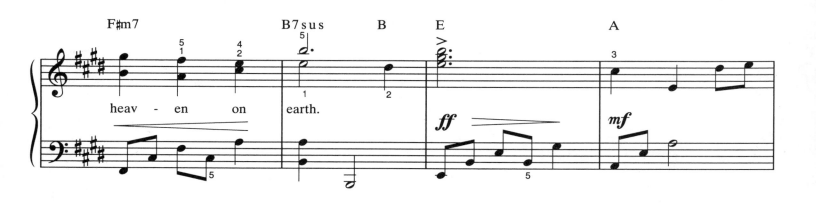

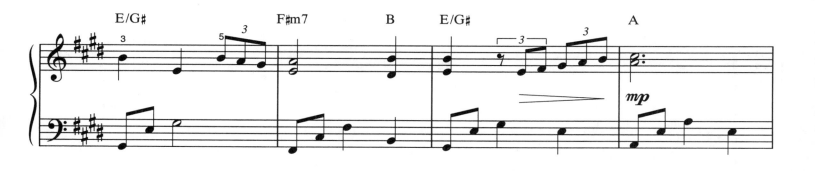

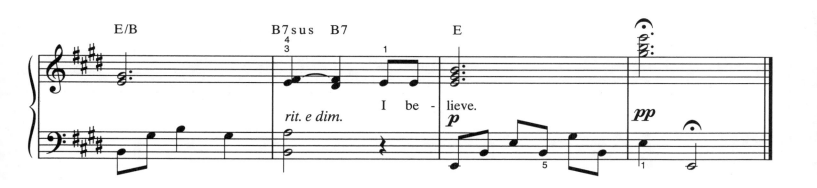

I Believe - 5 - 5

I THINK I'M IN LOVE WITH YOU

Words and Music by
MARK ROONEY, DAN SHEA
and JOHN MELLENCAMP
Arranged by DAN COATES

Bright dance tempo (♩ = 106)

I Think I'm in Love With You - 4 - 1

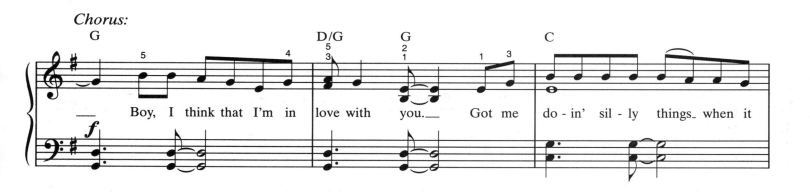

Chorus:

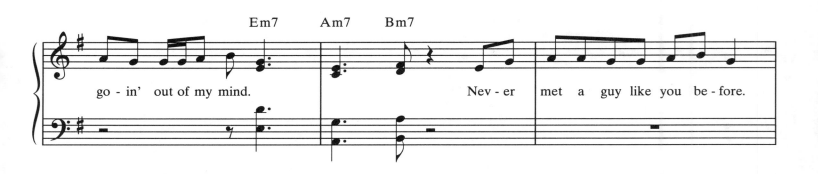

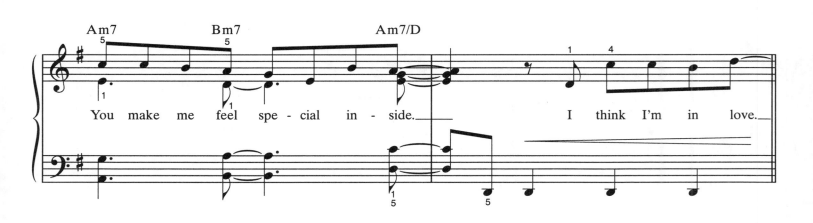

tell-in' all my friends what I feel for you.___ 2. Just the feel for you.___

Some-thing strange has come o-ver me.___ Got me

go-in' out of my mind. Nev-er met a guy like you be-fore.

You make me feel spe-cial in-side.___ I think I'm in love.___

Boy, I think that I'm in love with you.__ Got me do - in' sil - ly things__ when it

comes to you.__ Boy, I think that I'm in love with you.__ Got me

tell - in' all my friends__ what I feel for you.__ I'm in love.__ __

Verse 2:
Just the other night, baby,
I saw you hangin'.
You were with your crew.
I was with mine, too.
You took me by surprise
When you turned and looked me
In my eyes.
Oh, you really blew my mind.
I don't know what's gotten into me,
But I kinda think I know what it is.
I think I'm in love.
(To Chorus:)

IT'S MY LIFE

Words and Music by
JON BON JOVI, RICHIE SAMBORA
and MAX MARTIN
Arranged by DAN COATES

Steady rock beat (♩ = 120)

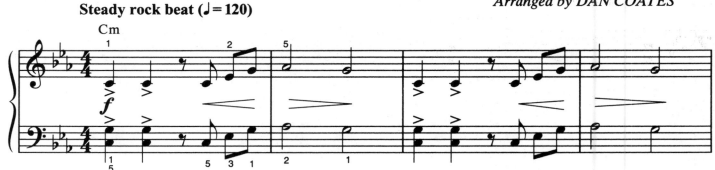

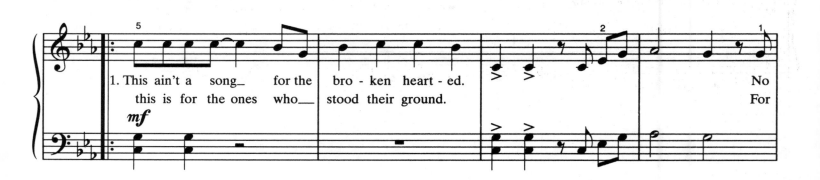

1. This ain't a song___ for the bro - ken heart - ed.
this is for the ones who___ stood their ground.
No For

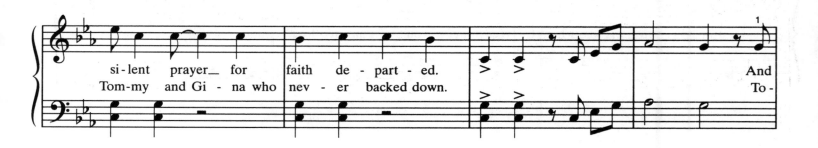

si - lent prayer___ for faith de - part - ed.
Tom - my and Gi - na who nev - er backed down.
And To -

I ain't gon - na be just a face in the crowd. You're gon - na hear my voice when I
mor - row's get - ting hard - er, make no mis - take.___ Luck ain't e - ven luck - y, got to

It's My Life - 4 - 1

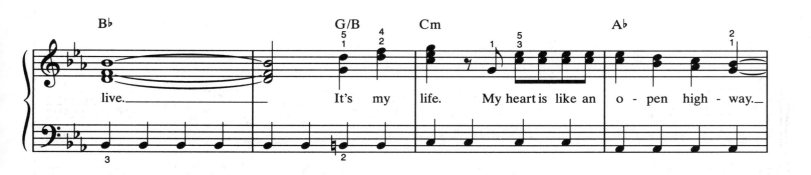

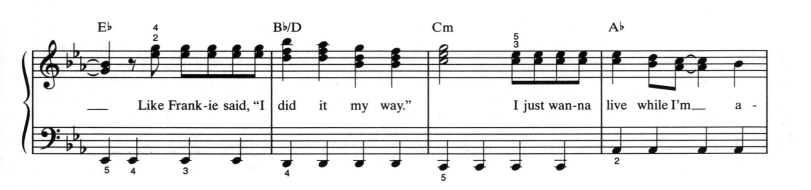

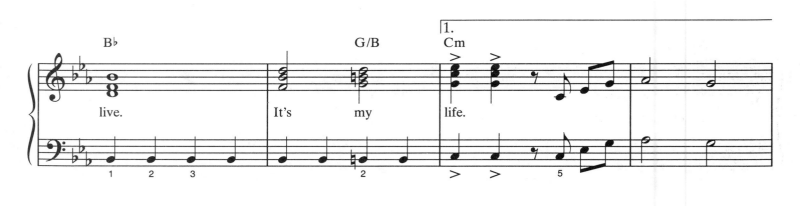

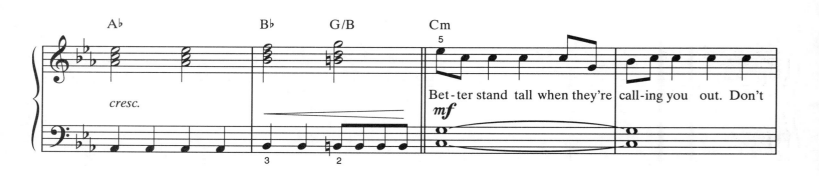

_ or nev - er._ Well, I ain't gon-na live for-ev - er. I just wan-na

live while I'm_ a - live._ It's my life. My heart is like an

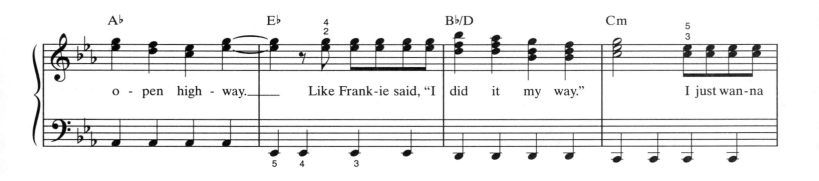

o - pen high - way._ Like Frank-ie said, "I did it my way." I just wan-na

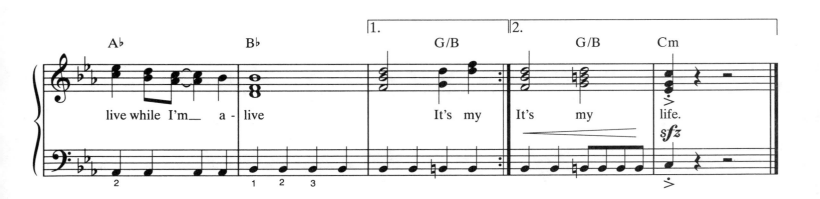

live while I'm_ a - live It's my It's my life.

KRYPTONITE

Words and Music by
**MATT ROBERTS, BRAD ARNOLD
and TODD HARRELL**
Arranged by RICHARD BRADLEY

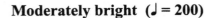

Moderately bright ($\quarternote$ = 200)

with pedal

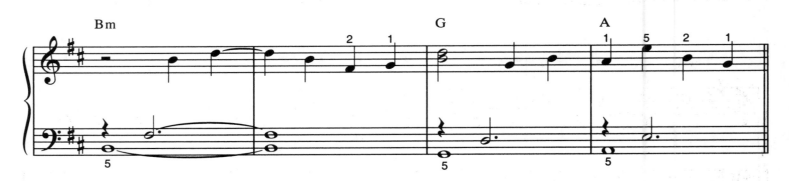

1. Well, I took a walk a-round the world to ease my trou-bled mind.

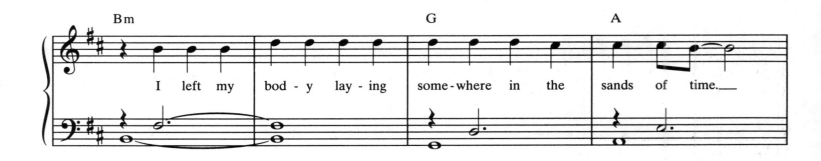

I left my bod-y lay-ing some-where in the sands of time.

Kryptonite - 6 - 1

And I watched the world___ float to the dark side of the moon.

And I feel there's noth-ing I can do. Yeah!

2. I watched the world___ float to the dark side of the moon.___

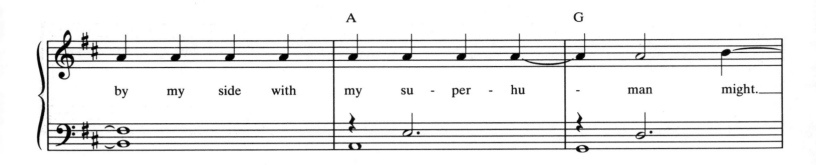

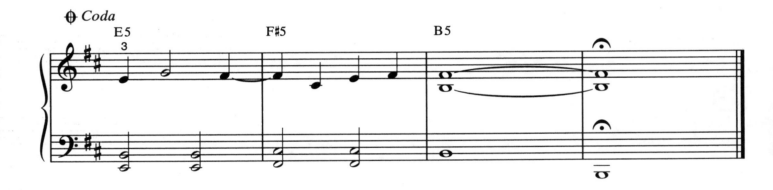

Verse 3:
You called me strong, you called me weak,
But still your secrets I keep.
You took for granted all the times I never let you down.
You stumbled in and bumped your head,
If not for me, then you would be dead.
I picked you up and put you back on solid ground.
(To Chorus:)

I TURN TO YOU

Words and Music by
DIANE WARREN
Arranged by DAN COATES

Slowly (♩ = 76)

% *Chorus:*

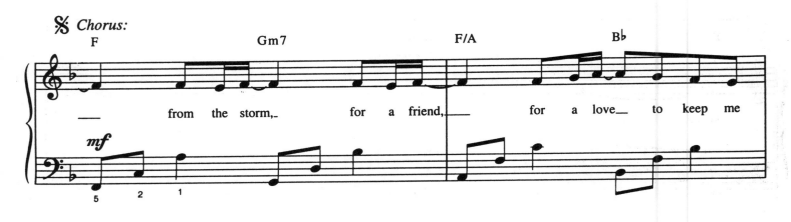

from the storm,— for a friend,— for a love— to keep me

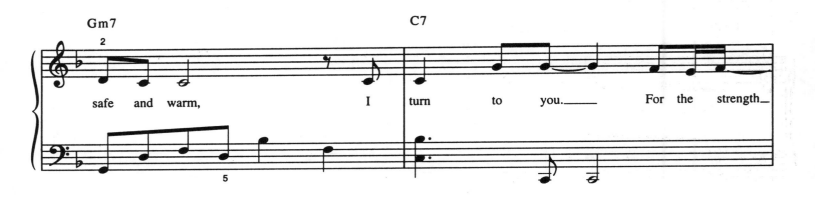

safe and warm, I turn to you.—— For the strength—

To Coda ⊕

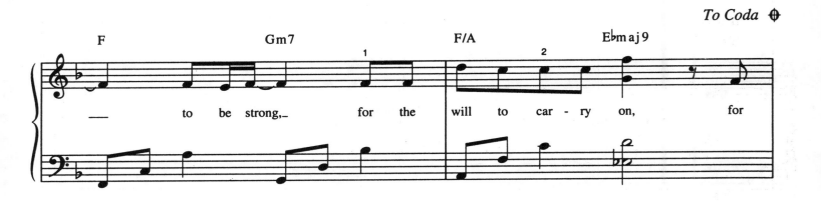

— to be strong,— for the will to car-ry on, for

1.

ev-'ry-thing— you do, for ev-'ry-thing— that's true, I turn to

F   Db/Eb   C7sus

you._____   2. When   I   lose___

mp

2.

Gm7   C7sus   F

ev - 'ry - thing___ you do, I turn to   you.

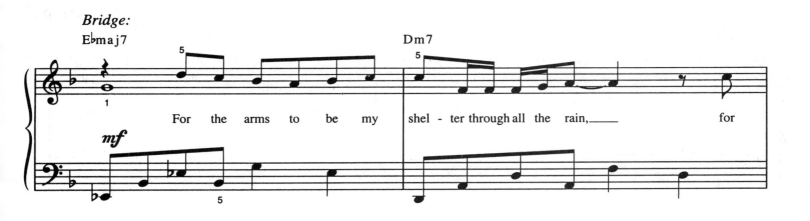

Bridge:

Ebmaj7   Dm7

For the arms to be my   shel - ter through all the rain,_____   for

mf

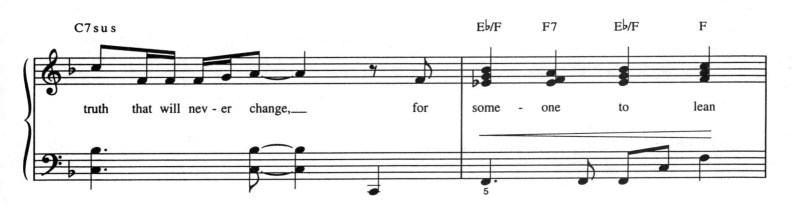

C7sus   Eb/F   F7   Eb/F   F

truth   that will nev - er change,___   for   some - one   to   lean

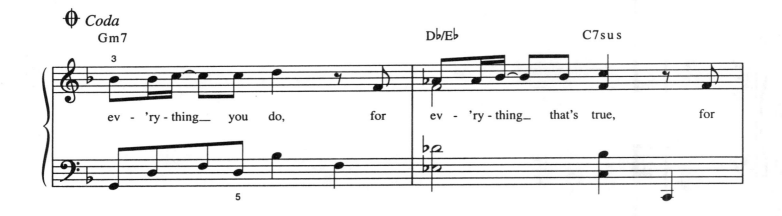

THE LITTLE GIRL

Words and Music by
HARLEY ALLEN
Arranged by DAN COATES

Moderately slow ballad (♩ = 88)

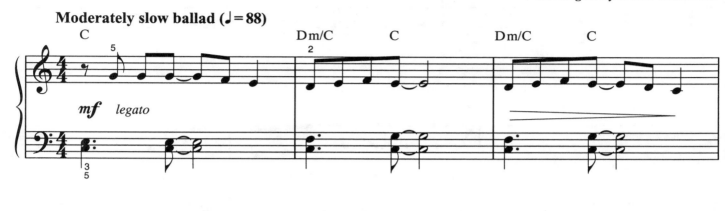

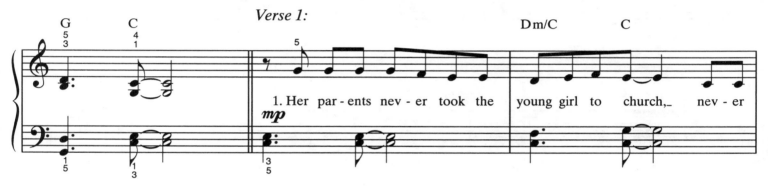

Verse 1:

1. Her par-ents nev-er took the young girl to church,_ nev-er

spoke of His name,_ nev-er read her His word._ Two non-be-liev-ers walk-ing

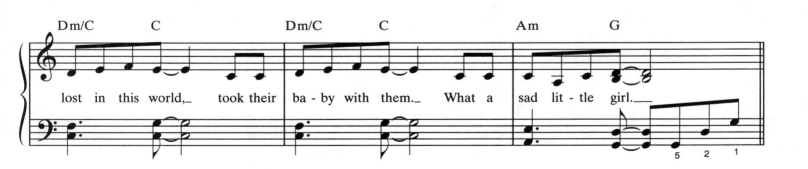

lost in this world,_ took their ba-by with them._ What a sad lit-tle girl._

The Little Girl - 3 - 1

66

The Little Girl - 3 - 2

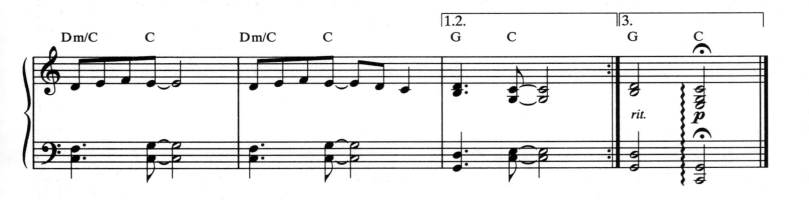

Verse 3:
And like it always does, the bad just got worse,
With every slap and every curse.
Until her daddy, in a drunk rage one night,
Used a gun on her mom and then took his life.

Chorus 2:
And some people from the city
Took the girl far away
To a new mom and a new dad,
Kisses and hugs every day.

Verse 4:
Her first day of Sunday school, the teacher walked in,
And a small little girl stared at a picture of Him.
She said, "I know that man up there on that cross.
I don't know his name, but I know he got off."

Chorus 3:
"'Cause He was there in my old house
And held me close to His side
As I hid there behind our couch
The night that my parents died."

A LOVE UNTIL
THE END OF TIME

Lyric by
CAROL CONNORS

Music by
LEE HOLDRIDGE
Arranged by DAN COATES

A Love Until the End of Time - 3 - 1

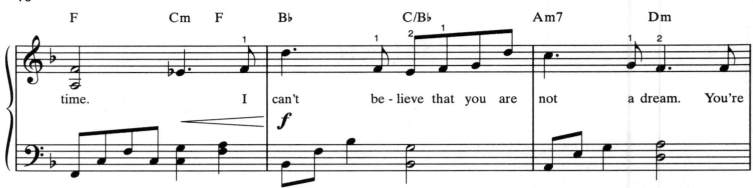

MUSIC

Words and Music by
MADONNA CICCONE and
MIRWAIS AHMADZAÏ
Arranged by RICHARD BRADLEY

Moderately fast (♩ = 120)

Music - 5 - 1

omit on D.S.

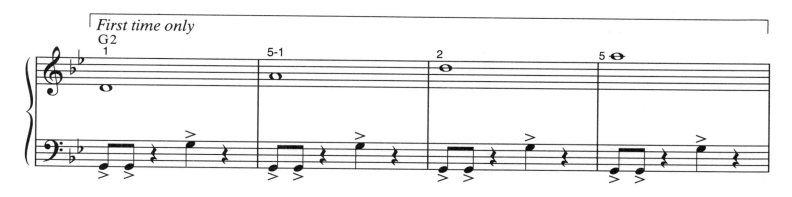

Hey,   Mis-ter   D   J.

D.S.%al Coda

(Nev - er   gon - na   stop.)

⊕ *Coda*

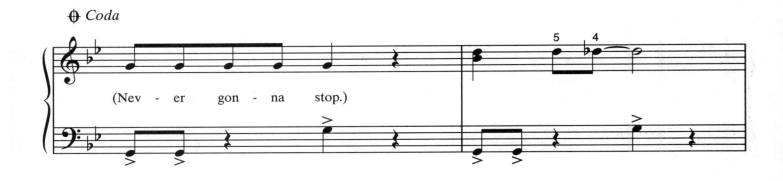

(Nev - er   gon - na   stop.)

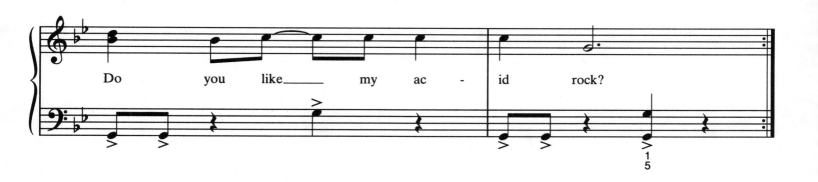

Verse 2:
Don't think of yesterday and I don't look at the clock.
I like to boogie woogie.
It's like riding on the wind and it never goes away,
Touches everything I'm in, got to have it every day.
(To Chorus:)

LUCKY

Words and Music by
MAX MARTIN, RAMI
and ALEXANDER KRONLUND
Arranged by DAN COATES

Moderate, steady beat (♩ = 96)

Verse 1:

1. Ear - ly morn-ing, she wakes up. Knock, knock, knock on the door.

It's time for make-up, per-fect smile. It's you they're all wait-ing for. They go,

Chorus:

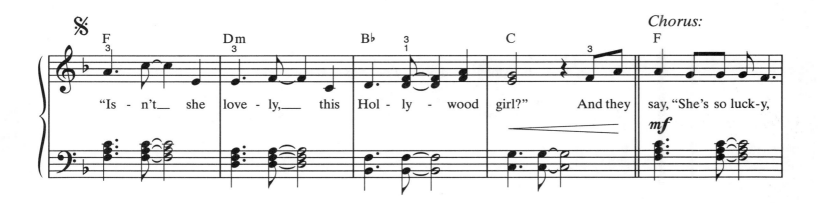

"Is - n't she love - ly, this Hol - ly - wood girl?" And they say, "She's so luck-y,

Lucky - 4 - 1

Dm

she's a star." But she cry, cry, cries in her lone - ly___ heart, think - ing,

Dm F/C B♭

if there's noth - ing miss - ing in my life, then why do___ these

To Coda ✛ *Verse 2:*

C7 F Dm

tears come___ at night? 2. Lost in an im - age, in a dream, but there's

mp

F Dm F

no one there to wake her up. And the world is spin - ning and she

D.S. 𝄋 al Coda

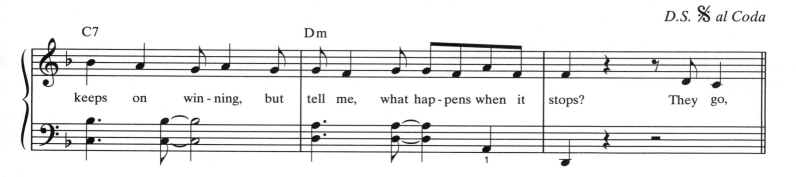

C7 Dm

keeps on win - ning, but tell me, what hap - pens when it stops? They go,

noth - ing___ miss - ing in her life, why do tears come___ at night?

Chorus:

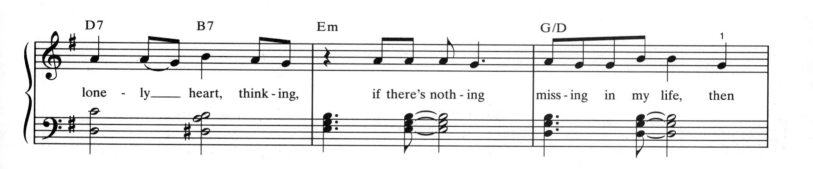

mf "She's so luck - y, she's a star." But she cry, cry, cries in her

lone - ly___ heart, think - ing, if there's noth - ing miss - ing in my life, then

why do___ these tears come___ at night? tears come___ at night?

MY EVERYTHING

Words and Music by
ARNTHOR BIRGISSON, ANDERS SVEN BAGGE,
NICK LACHEY and ANDREW LACHEY
Arranged by DAN COATES

Slowly, with expression
Verse:

(with pedal throughout)

1. The lone - li - ness_ of nights_ so long,_ the search for strength_ to car - ry on._ My ev - 'ry hope_ had seemed_ to die,_ my eyes had no_ more tears_
all my hopes_ and all_ my dreams_ are sud - den - ly_ re - al - i - ty._ You've o-pened up_ my heart to feel_ a kind of love_ that's tru -

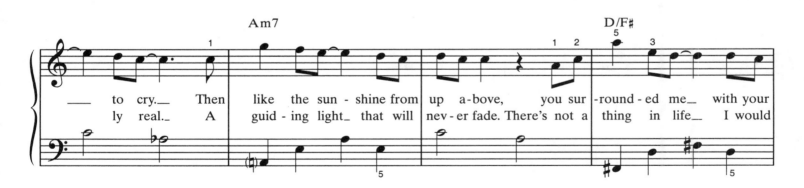

_ to cry._ Then like the sun - shine from up a-bove, you sur -round - ed me_ with your end-less love. And all the things_ I could - n't see are now so clear to
ly real._ A guid - ing light_ that will nev - er fade. There's not a thing in life_ I would ev - er trade. For the love you give_ and won't let go, I hope you'll al - ways

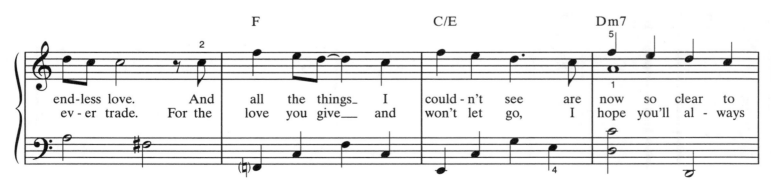

Chorus:

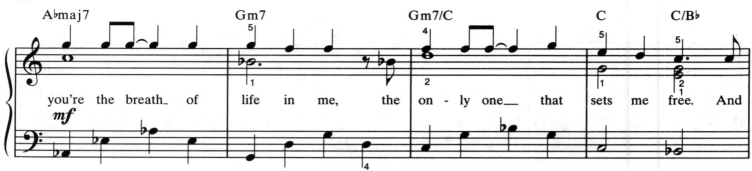

you're the breath_ of life in me, the on - ly one__ that sets me free. And

you have made_ my soul com - plete for all time. You are my

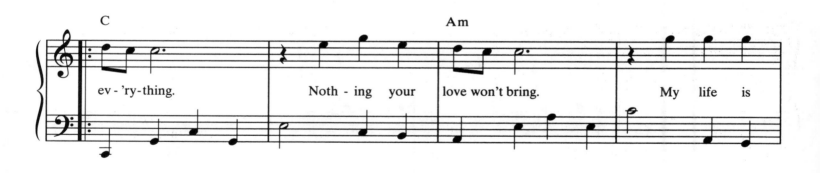

ev - 'ry-thing. Noth - ing your love won't bring. My life is

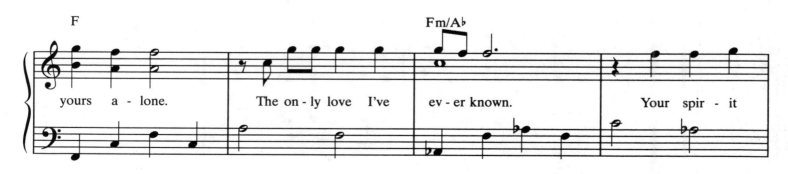

yours a - lone. The on - ly love I've ev - er known. Your spir - it

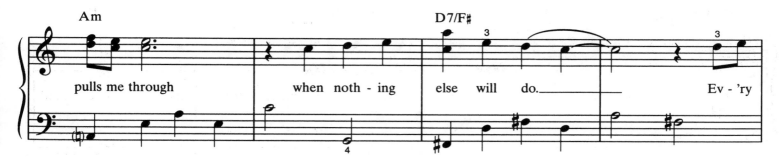

Am ... D7/F#

pulls me through — when noth - ing else will do.___ Ev - 'ry

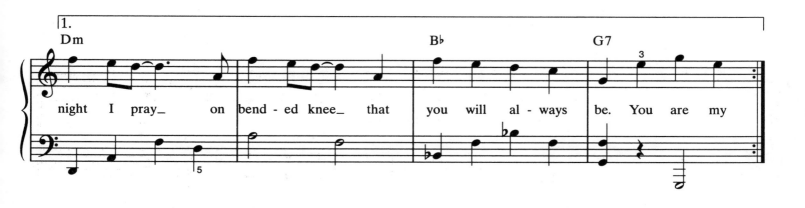

1.

Dm ... B♭ ... G7

night I pray_ on bend - ed knee_ that you will al - ways be. You are my

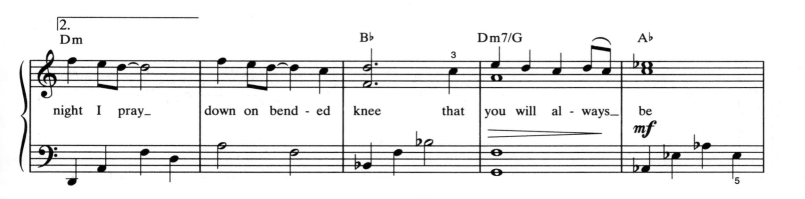

2.

Dm ... B♭ ... Dm7/G ... A♭

night I pray_ down on bend - ed knee that you will al - ways_ be

mf

B♭ ... C

my ev - 'ry - thing, oh, my ev - e - ry - thing.

rit. e dim.

mp

p

My Everything - 4 - 4

NEED TO BE NEXT TO YOU

Words and Music by
DIANE WARREN
Arranged by DAN COATES

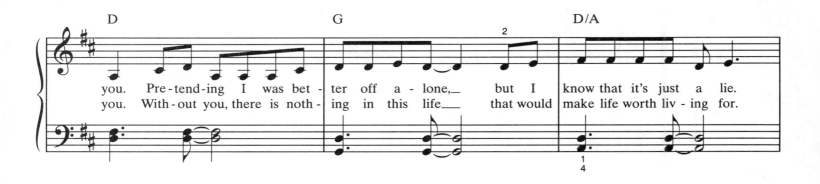

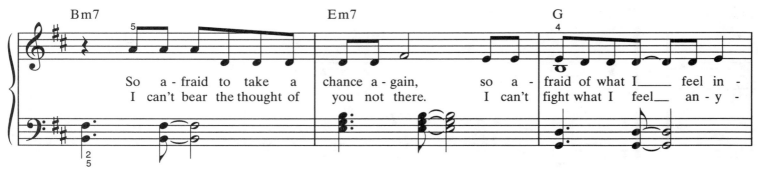

Need to Be Next to You - 4 - 1

Chorus:

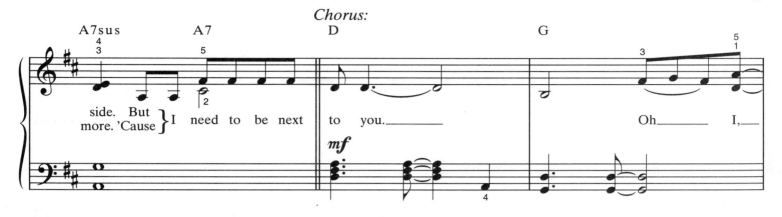

side. But
more. 'Cause } I need to be next to you.___ Oh___ I,

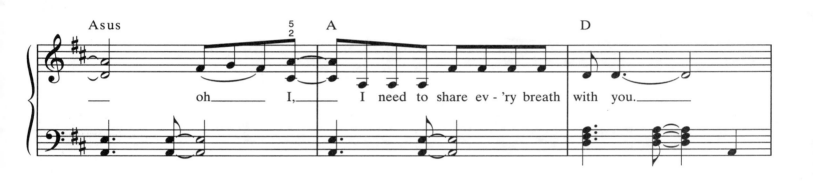

___ oh___ I,___ I need to share ev-'ry breath with you.___

Oh___ I,___ oh___ I,___ I need to know I can see

your smile each morn-ing, look in-to your eyes each night___ for the rest of___ my___

86

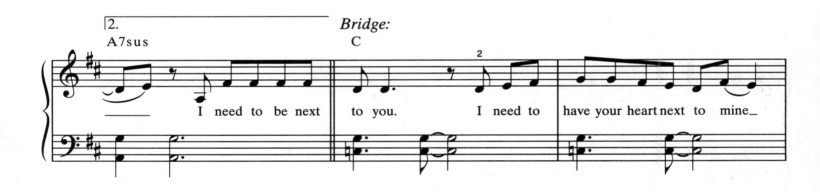

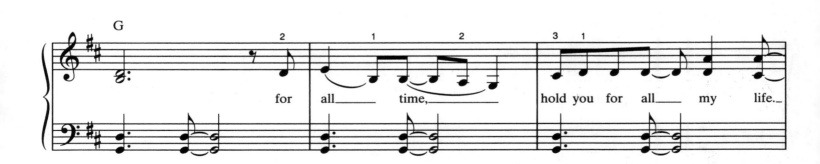

SHAPE OF MY HEART

Words and Music by
MAX MARTIN, RAMI
and LISA MISKOVSKY
Arranged by DAN COATES

Moderately slow (♩ = 96)

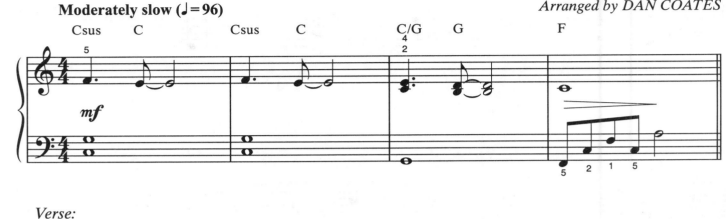

Verse:

1. Ba - by,___ please try___ to for - give me.___
2. Sad - ness is beau - ti - ful.___ Lone - li - ness is

trag - i - cal.___ So Stay here,___ don't put out the___ glow.
help me,___ I can't win this___ war.

Hold me now,___ don't both -
Touch me now,___ don't both -

Shape of My Heart - 4 - 1

Chorus:

Shape of My Heart - 4 - 2

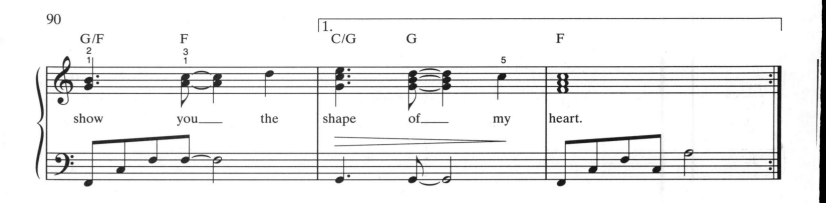

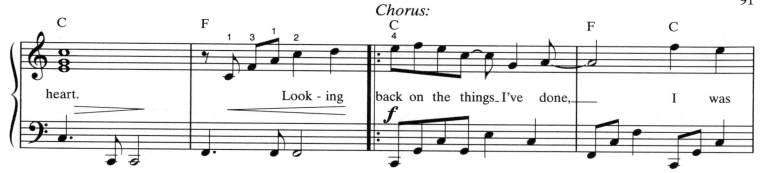

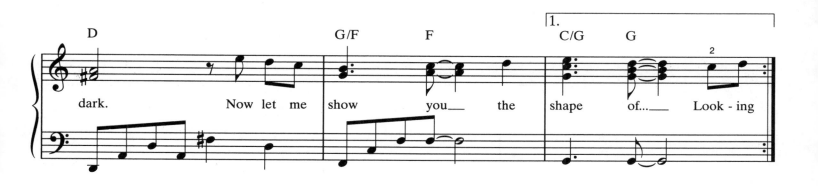

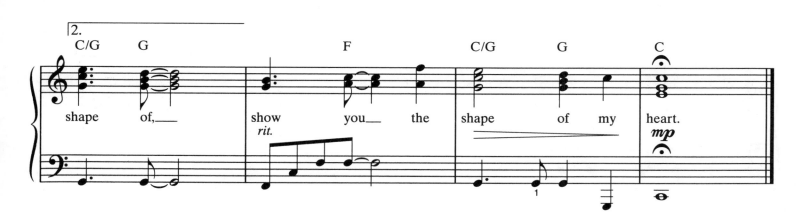

STRONGER

Words and Music by
MAX MARTIN and **RAMI**
Arranged by DAN COATES

Moderately, with a strong beat ($\bf{\bullet}$ = 108)

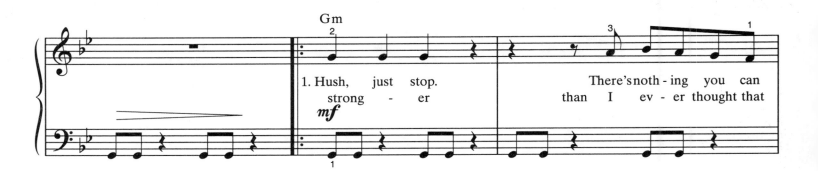

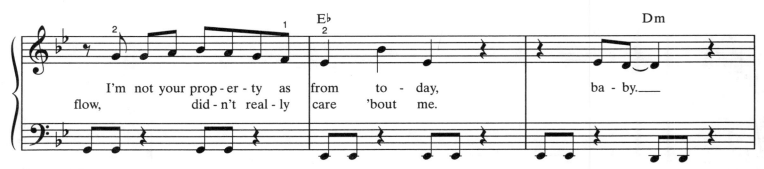

Stronger - 4 - 1

Oh, yeah.___ Here I go, on my own. I don't

need no-bod-y, bet-ter off a-lone. Here I go,___ on my own now.

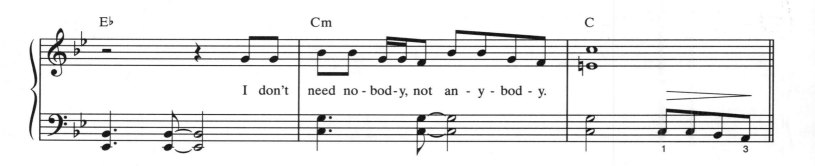

Eb　　　　　　　　　Cm　　　　　　　　　C

I don't need no-bod-y, not an-y-bod-y.

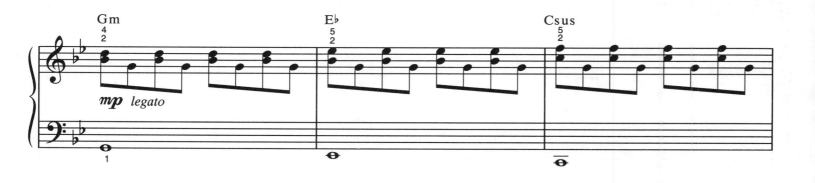

Gm　　　　　　　　　Eb　　　　　　　　　Csus

mp legato

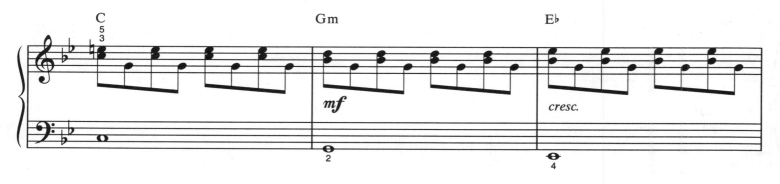

C　　　　　　　　　Gm　　　　　　　　　Eb

mf　　　　　　　　　cresc.

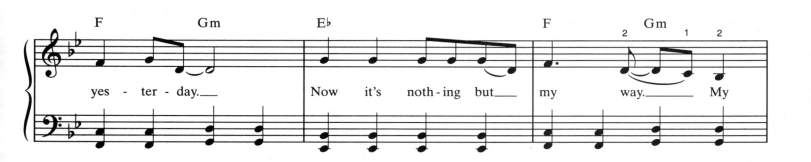

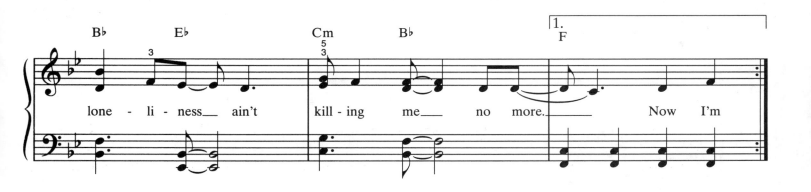

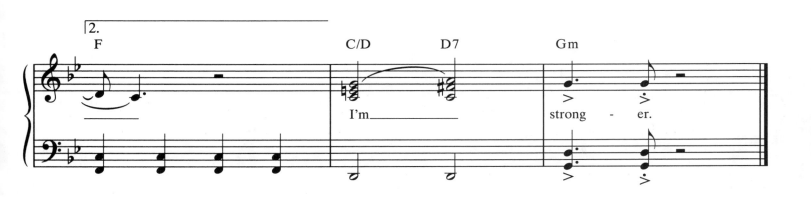

THANK YOU FOR LOVING ME

Words and Music by
JON BON JOVI and RICHIE SAMBORA
Arranged by DAN COATES

Slowly (♩ = 66)

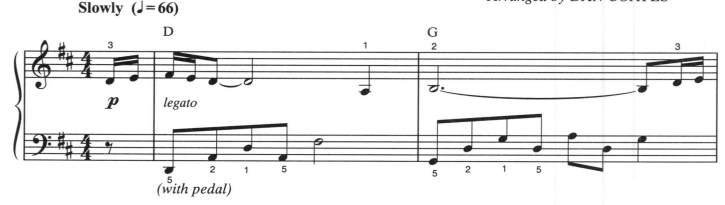

Verse:

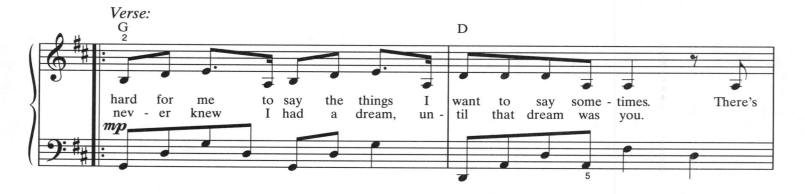

hard for me to say the things I want to say some-times. There's
nev-er knew I had a dream, un-til that dream was you.

no one here but you and me and that bro-ken old street light. Lock the
When I look in-to your eyes, the sky's a dif-f'rent blue. Cross my

Thank You for Loving Me - 4 - 1

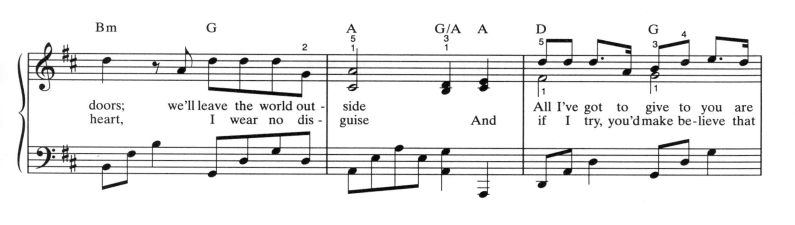

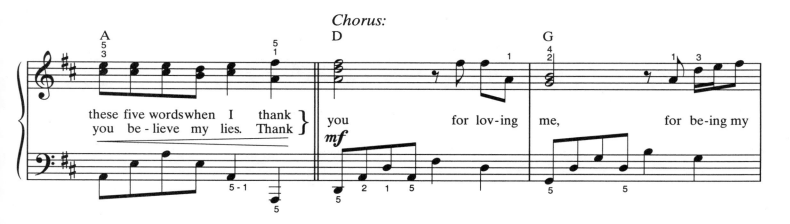

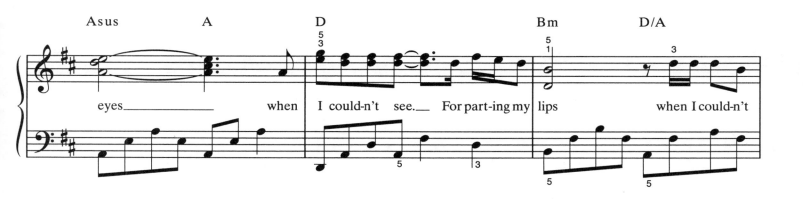

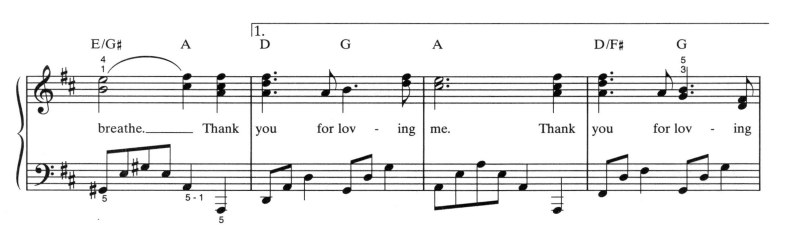

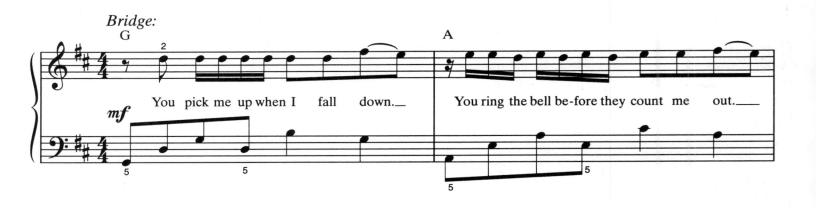

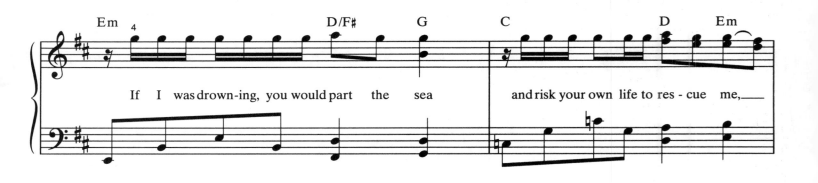

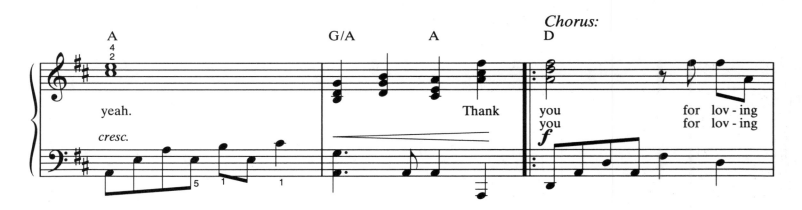

THIS I PROMISE YOU

Words and Music by
RICHARD MARX
Arranged by DAN COATES

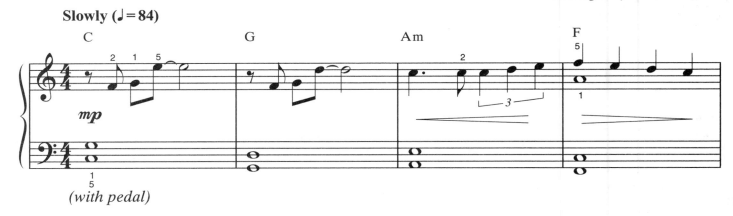

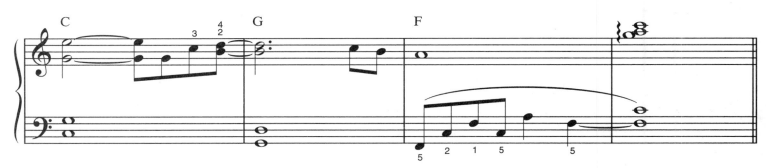

This I Promise You - 4 - 1

SHE BANGS

Words and Music by
ROBI ROSA, WALTER AFANASIEFF
and DESMOND CHILD
Arranged by RICHARD BRADLEY

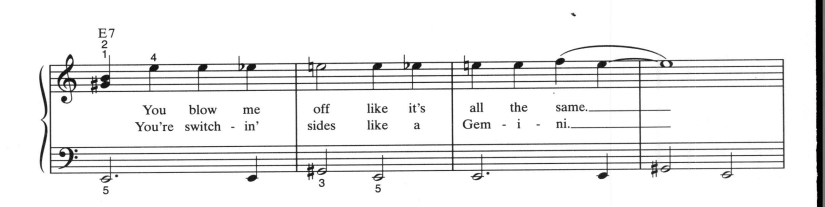

She Bangs - 5 - 1

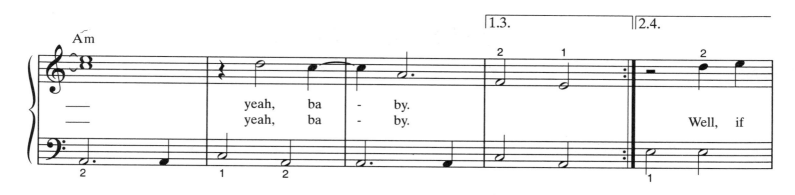

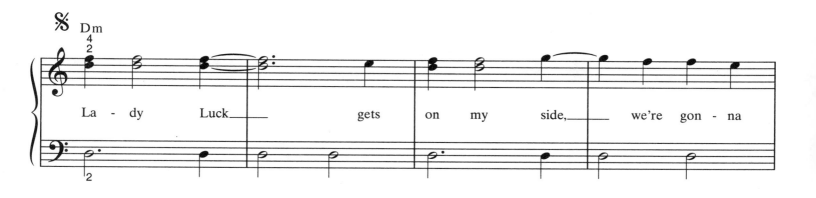

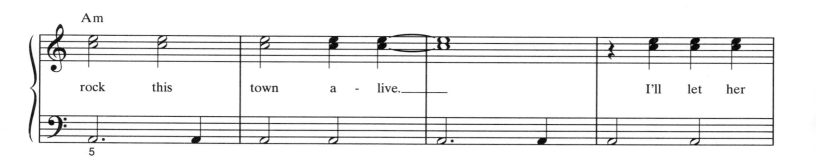

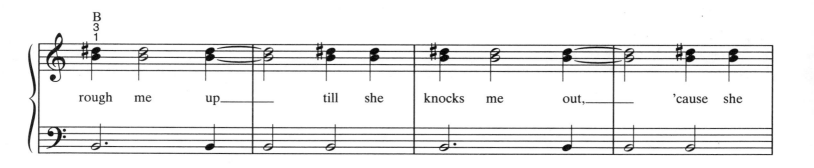

She Bangs - 5 - 2

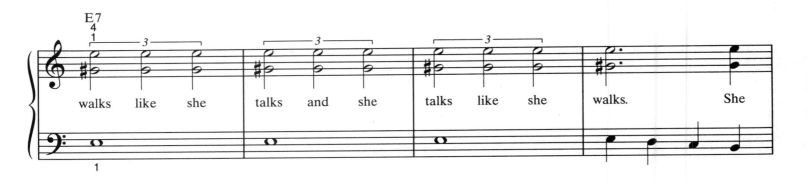

walks   like   she   talks   and   she   talks   like   she   walks.   She

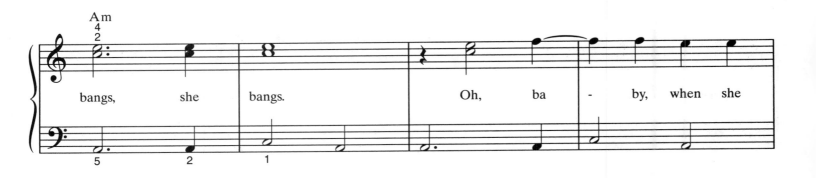

bangs,   she   bangs.   Oh,   ba - by,   when   she

moves,   she   moves.   I   go   cra - zy   'cause   she

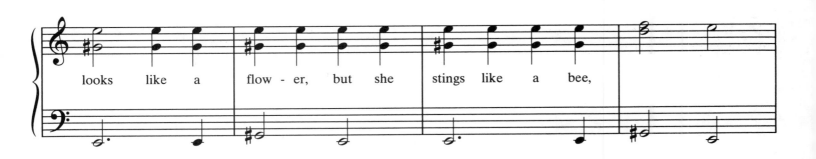

looks   like   a   flow - er,   but   she   stings   like   a   bee,

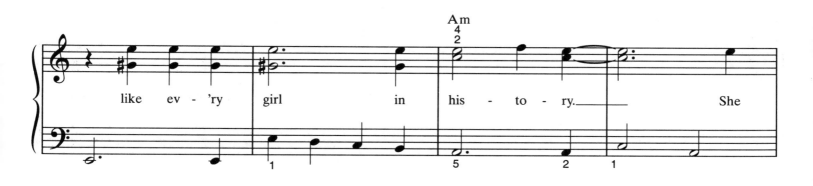

like ev - 'ry girl in his - to - ry._____ She

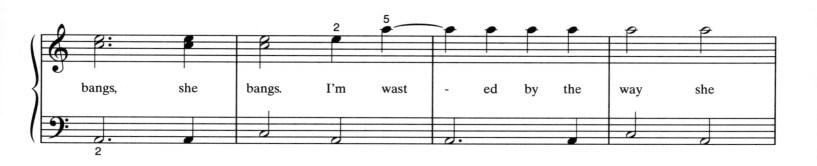

bangs, she bangs. I'm wast - ed by the way she

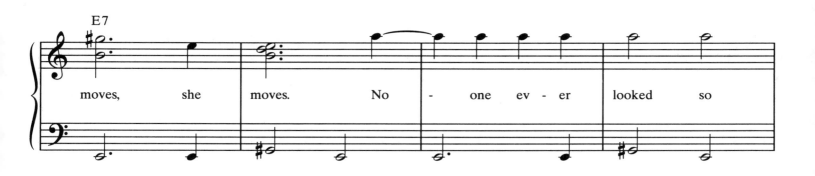

moves, she moves. No - one ev - er looked so

fine. She re - minds_____ me that a

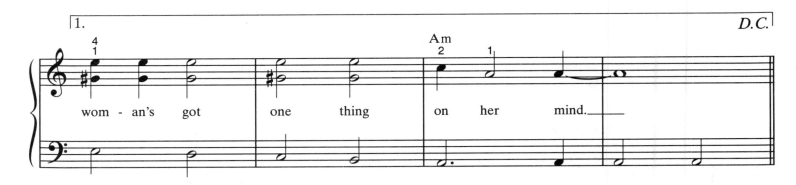

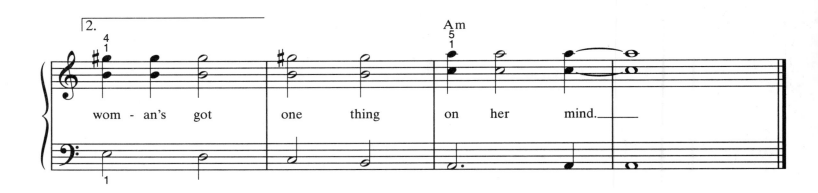

Verse 3:
Talk to me, tell me your name.
I'm just a link in your daisy chain.
Your rap sounds like a diamond map
To the stars, yeah, baby.

Verse 4:
Talk to me, tell me the news.
You'll wear me out like a pair of shoes.
We'll dance until the band goes home,
Then you're gone, yeah, baby.
Well, if it looks like love should be a crime,
You'd better lock me up for life.
I'll do the time with a smile on my face,
Thinkin' of her in her leather and lace.

WIN

Words and Music by
BRIAN McNIGHT and BRANDON BARNES
Arranged by DAN COATES

Moderately slow (♩ = 64)

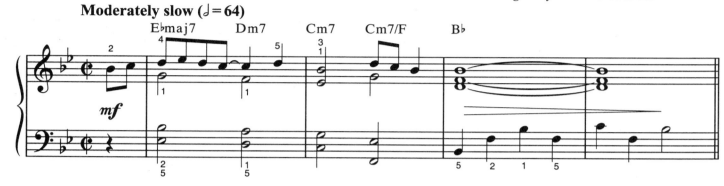

Verse:

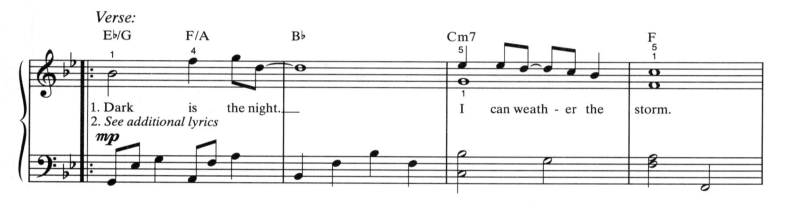

1. Dark is the night.___ I can weath - er the storm.
2. *See additional lyrics*

Nev - er say die.___ I've been down this road_ be - fore. I'll nev - er

quit, I'll nev - er break down. See, I

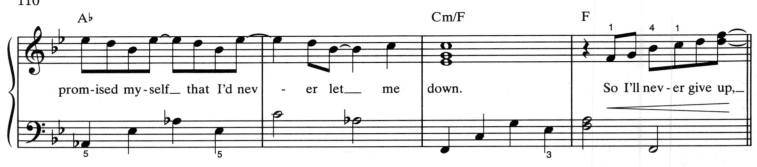

Chorus:

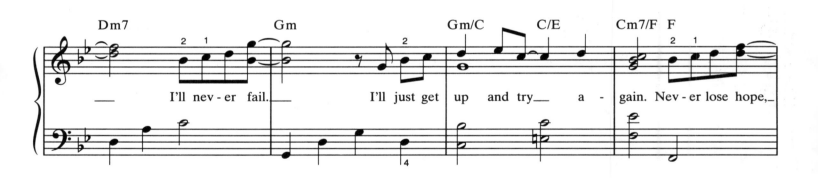

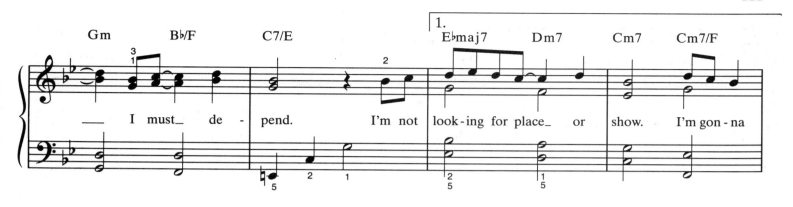

Gm   B♭/F   C7/E   **1.** E♭maj7   Dm7   Cm7   Cm7/F

— I must__ de - pend.   I'm not look-ing for place_ or show.   I'm gon-na

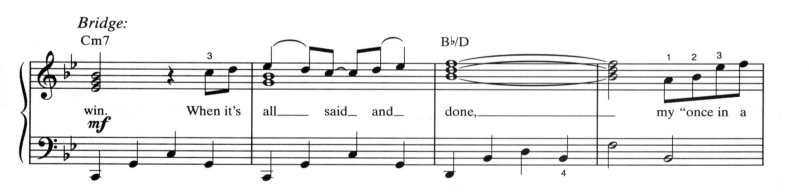

B♭   **2.** E♭maj7   Dm7   Cm7   Cm7/F

win._____   look-ing for place_ or show.   I'm gon-na

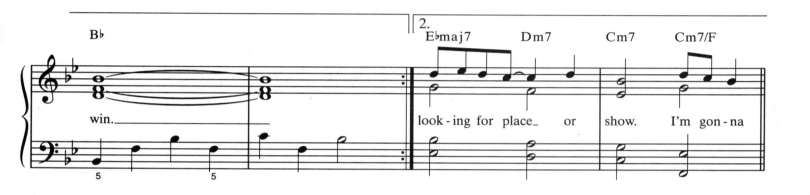

Bridge:
Cm7   B♭/D

win. *mf*   When it's all__ said__ and__ done,_____   my "once in a

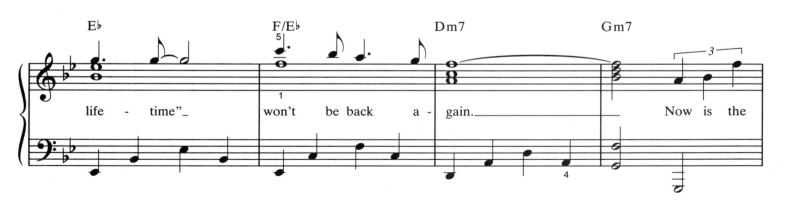

E♭   F/E♭   Dm7   Gm7

life - time"_   won't be back a - gain._____   Now is the

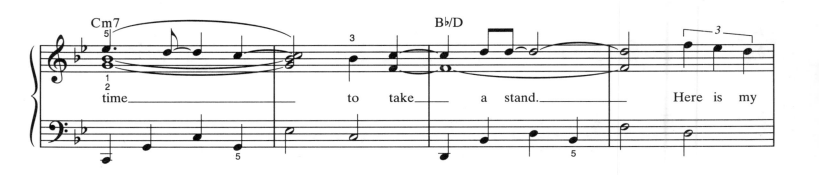

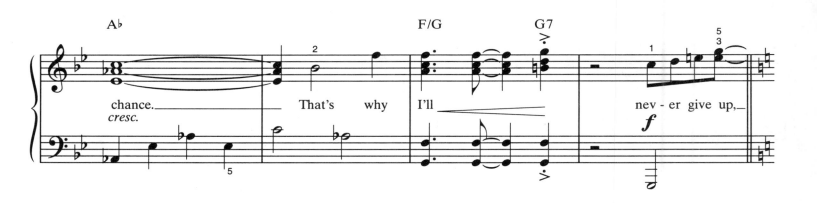

nev - er lose faith.___ There's much___ too much___ at stake.___ Up - on___ my - self

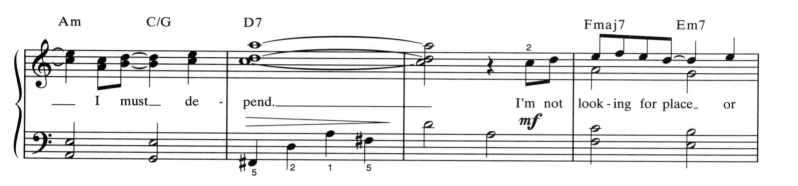

___ I must___ de - pend._____ I'm not look - ing for place___ or

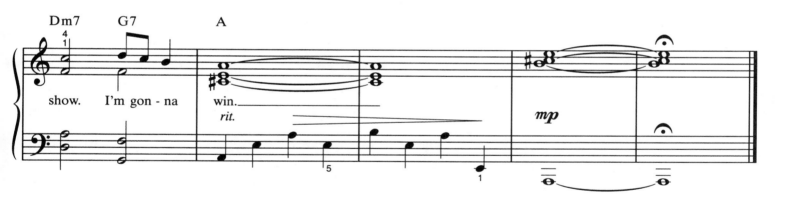

show. I'm gon - na win.___

Verse 2:
No stopping now,
There's still a ways to go.
Some way, somehow,
Whatever it takes, I know
I'll never quit.
I'll never go down.
I'll make sure they remember my name
A hundred years from now.
(To Chorus:)

Win - 5 - 5

WWW.MEMORY

Words and Music by
ALAN JACKSON
Arranged by RICHARD BRADLEY

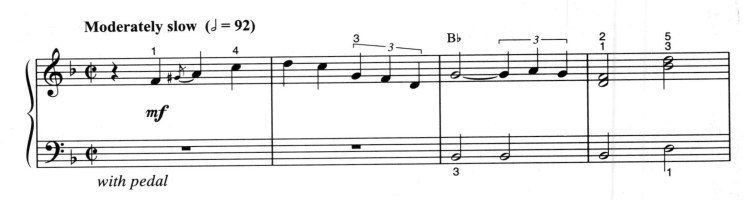

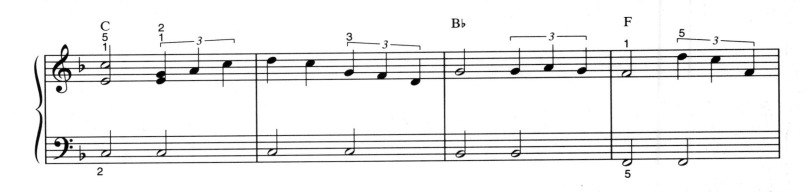

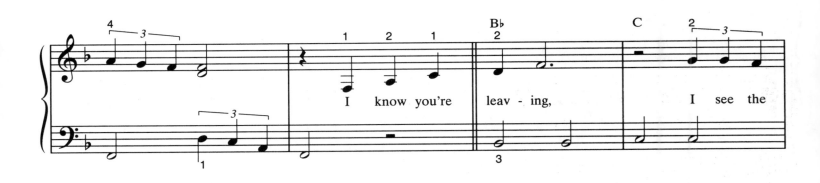

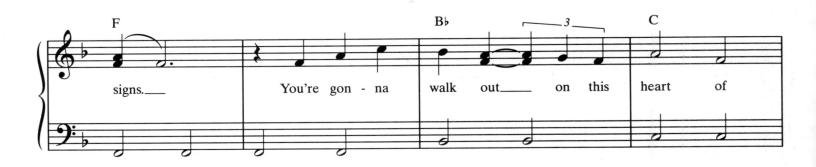

118

WHERE ARE YOU CHRISTMAS?

Words and Music by
JAMES HORNER, WILL JENNINGS
and MARIAH CAREY
Arranged by DAN COATES

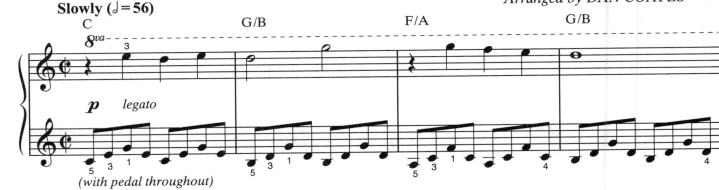

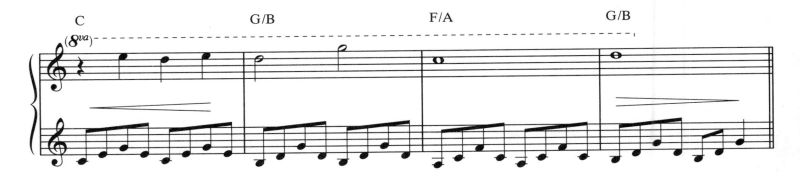

Verse 1:

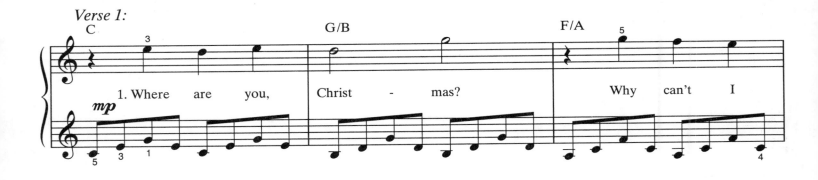

Where Are You Christmas? - 5 - 2

Where Are You Christmas? - 5 - 3

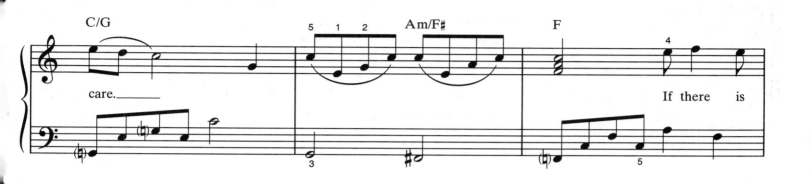

care._____ If there is

love in your heart and your mind,

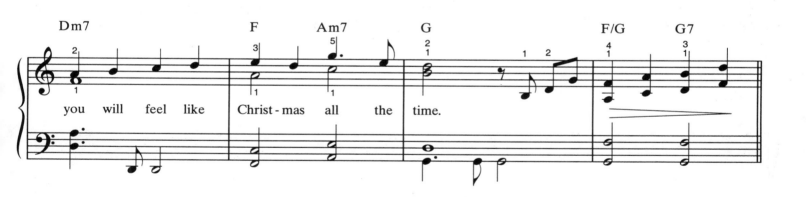

you will feel like Christ-mas all the time.

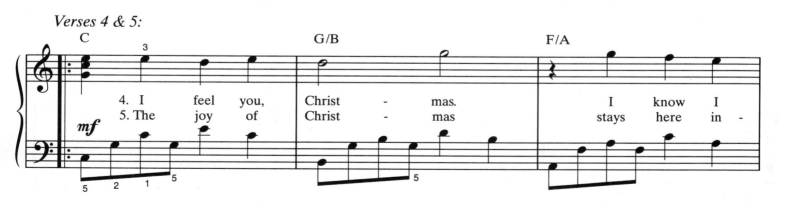

Verses 4 & 5:

4. I feel you, Christ - mas. I know I
5. The joy of Christ - mas stays here in -

mf